Standards of Sadiddy

Standards of Sadiddy

Jonathan Penton

ISBN: 978-1-943170-18-0

Cover Art: © Amy Guidry
Cover Design: Jane L. Carman
Interior Design: Jane L. Carman and Jonathan Penton

Typefaces: Arial, Garamond, Gothic Ultra, and Palatino Linotype

Published by: Lit Fest Press, Carman, 688 Knox Road 900 North, Gilson, Illinois 61436

Lit Fest Press

No rules. No pants.
festivalwriter.org

Dedicated to the memory of
Kurtice Kucheman, May 31, 1981–February 23, 2014
and
Michelle Greenblatt, August 21, 1982–October 19, 2015

two of the finest friends and thinkers I could ever hope to know

Contents

Charles Bukowski's Greatest Mistake

Coffee by day, tequila by night
    clear the putty from the washing machine hose
    change the lock on the daughter's door
    argue your parking rights with the city employee
    tell the neighbor why his cousin's in jail

The computers you hated talk back to us now
    bills you avoided come in a 'Net made of gold
    lovers strategize like a mayor on parole
        we no longer notice when we go to War

            it is *War All The Time*
            it always was

        When *Bukowski Tapes* are rolling
        We are all beating your woman
        Though we aren't too young for justice
        And won't grow too old for chaos
        You were always full of shit

        That shit that always hits the fan

Still you can spot a pacifist
when he won't quit after the armistice
'cause every poet's just a militant
looking for a weapon he won't have to put down

It is your War, Charles Bukowski
We lost when you forgot it was on

The Way Buckeyes and Buds Taste Just Like the Lone Star

So the ink-stained asphalt stretched before me
      'neath that dotted yellow line
sleeping like a leather domme who never looks inside

and the stars came out to celebrate my reminiscing
in every place that is deserted, all the places that are brave

once   i saw
      a thousand points of light when all the cigarettes could
      burn in unison

so i sat down with a Raleigh in Montezuma's bed
to dream the sweet hard heart of Staten Island on game night

      i wrapped   my lips
         'round Indians east and west
         who tried to teach me to love
         folks who weren't like me

then sank   my thumbs
      into Schenectadian mud
      back to when i never loved no folks at all

           i don't mean to get political

it's just great-uncle Jack told us to travel like a child
even after Burroughs shot that hole in gramma's head

What the Roads Are Paved With

i tell myself it matters what i notice
that be i pardoned or be punished

                    reflection gives our tale some depth
i act as though an inner deity observes

                    judging the banal self-analyses
                    behind the toy box on your shelf

i write as though cruelty could have a context
my invocation of cliché imbues me with a right

although it is a   waste

              of time

                  to chronicle this madness

it is equally foolish
to try to catalogue the sane   who sit

              with

                their birthdays
                and their

        no-truths-outside-of-things

when there's a common fire inside my body
      laughing at public soliloquies
how the sure thing crumbles in Los Angelean slime like
         forgetting,
           like forgetting,
              like the sole purpose of memory

like the way our heart's intention is to find a way to stop

do you remember the night
he called you names?

do you remember the names he called you
the names you called you
names you struggled so hard to abandon
      worked so hard to earn?

     now you're fragile as a straight flush,
counting and writing backwards,
      erecting your defenses in your Empire's Building of State
like that torch-wielding seamstress who knows only she has power
      to spite the tourists and New Havenites pedaling in the park

turning your skin to Pepto-Bismol since your heart will always burn

can you remember the truth behind the mania
      before civility and sympathy made you competent
      at the interactions you know don't matter

before adulthood found you burying the furies you need most

Every Day of Her Life
for Yetta Rose

Once she ate from the tree of good and evil
sometimes she knew which she preferred
once she played a karmic agent
on a dance floor with a handgun

She laughs at your professions of sentience
since she fed your soul to her dog
she mocks the colored nurses who don't scare her in the slightest

'cause they're
   looking for meaning in profits and pendants
or the doctors, the patients, her memories made of metaphor
   the gibberish with which she speaks forthright

Her brothers are terrified
her son still needs to suffer
though she's told them that it's just a waste of time
so she learns to hunt for robin's eggs
and fling them from her branches
to prepare us for when we've lost our minds

perch atop this mountain built   with speed stick-flavored sweat
knowing one misstep will bring it down
plant one foot in the graves of those who forget you
and one foot on the children who don't care
take your shriveled cock
removed from eternity   as time will let it be
tell yourself it's better to resist gravity
that the thrill of impact is someone else's memory.

The Nunnery

we are building a religion but not all with the same gods
we are sleeping in this nunnery   where no   vow of silence   ever
meant   as   much   as the lunatic   pounding the piano
                    with a perfect sense of tempo
                                        but no desire for grace

the ringmaster is warning us of the dangers of gossip while
            sucking off the cultist who's got no place to stay
the opera singer's warning me not to wear my glasses 'cause
            the doctors are conspiring to eliminate my race

and i'm OK
it's a Lake Erie winter
but i have a mattress and a cell that's really quite warm
and i've got a couple 40s stored right outside this window
where the architecture rises like ten shorn drunks on minarets
tumbling toward Bethlehem against a bullet-ridden sigh
while your dreams stay in the basement where they kept
            the pregnant sisters
waiting for the capricious millennium to be born

North

the fields of tar are breaking
under copper-smelting towers
and you ask if you can cut me
to make our photos just pyrite

i grab hold of those fences
still formed from ocotillo
and i try to wrap up in them
but they don't think they're part of this
so don't do anything at all

we head east on Montana
back to your mother's bedroom
where she's laid out all her gris-gris in hope of keeping me away
you get out your tattoo gun
and you promise me Picasso
but it seems my back's forgotten
so my hands best push you anywhere but here
   where i can see the
      scar across your neck the one that
      tanglewebs   in all directions
like something no doctor has the fingertips to do

it seems my back has lost a great deal more than your tattoo gun
which didn't work much better than the spine you still must keep

outside, the dust storm is starting
the sun is falling down in daylight
we should scamper to lower ground
though we know we'll never make it
before the grey and brown surround the way
our eyes forget the sunset
our hands forget the how of when we
climbed those yielding rocks
those pieces pointed skyward
to see the tapestry of femicide
          a map of smallpox comforts
dust embedded in our teeth

'cause if my hands are forgetful
i think my mouth remembers
how you begged it to cut you
to get the Glamour Shot just right

i would have you die in beauty like a Fante heroine
so please-please when you read to me
          put down the Earnest Gaines.

Dream in Black and Red

Mother   you were silent
up against your pillows
        waiting for that baby you knew you could not save

and i wonder if your hopelessness
        brought you any freedom

        While we bustled in our ignorance
and Fabio-streaked ceilings
        While we monitored your bathroom trips
and tried our hands at pancakes
        while the doctors tried to tell us
gentle things we could not learn

from whom i ask the favor

i don't have a fortress
        i just have a paradox
        in which the devil cannot find a place
                to set down his ground rules
i hide in self-perception
        like the minotaur's hot breath
        proceeding from Blavatsky's table
                where she keeps the hand grenades

i call this security though i know how lost i am
        i call myself triumphant because this maze will outlive me
        standing naked as a heart attack
                between radiant leaves of weed

There's a child standing on that caliché skyscraper
Buried under a century of Simon and Garfunkel
He meant to come down, but there's a sun and a grandfather
Who can't remember why he came

The cameras are rolling, the point guards are throwing
        beads and poppers
        and rivers of whiskey and Phoenix
The glare from the streetlamps burns Ohio River bridges
        'til the tenderizing blast
        turns Ol' Miss into glass

So the Contras get desperate, Princess Di is protesting
Stevie Nicks and "Fireworks" and strip-mining Oasis
        and we're stretching these metaphors
        like ambulance-chasers trying to find truth in a song
                        though three-quarters time is wrong

We look back to the child on the school-lunch skyscraper
He's learned to flow fresh and roll blunts without fingers
His rhymes are compiled of waterboarding he learned from
The alliteration on porn mags

                He still classifies by race

So he's kept distracted from the son and the grandfather
While they melt the jello foundation of the skyscraper
Lest heavy metals allow him to avoid the decision
                to be or not to be
                        like Eszterhas watching *Buffy*

Pauline tells me she puts Kahlúa in her morning coffee,
sliding sensually into the day,
pondering the twelve words or so she might write in the afternoon

Norah, gluten-free and High German, prepares for two hours
at the jazz club with
ten hours in bed,
                    six ounces of feta,
a few nibbles of lettuce and innumerable unstained clothes

and i
        American
                    can't help but feel like Lolita
                                    surrounded by this
fat-thin decadence that leaves me hunting feral cats
screaming that midnight is for tequila and morning is for agony
and comfort is plain ugliness in a boundless, brutal land.

craving purity when i speak of craving people

my body claims i'm filled with tiny answers
my mouth tells you how i like to lie
i just have this 12-gauge air-filled needle
and hope i can mimic your silence while alive

It's a major moment, when a girl first falls in love with a pair of
shoes—we breathe, we relax, we appreciate, we know there's a
30% probability she's already developed her first fetish.

We are lightened by her joy, we feel the weight of winnowing—
We understand these white shoes mean she'll never learn to love
the red and we are

privileged to watch something morphous become Venus
to watch deity assert herself, set free from purer stuff
like that infant god who clawed out from his father's belly
and turned us into individuals when all we had was names

O   blessed ur-poem   archetype made flesh
You who know that all we other gods go forth but for your grace
Do you remember your dependency on those siblings
        who sprung forth
                those other pieces of your god-stuff
                with less sublime predilections
Who chose differently at those moments before choice
                                                became a joke

Notyu Journal II

this is the flipside of the focus
the way the word sylvan oppresses the green
the unnecessary punch line

Oh, for a unique delusion!
Let us pray for a muse of other than fire

you don't have to accept anything
your rebellion is as good as any other
heroism is always misplaced anyway

If this is, in fact, a post-patriarchy
the sort commercialism can keep afloat
Never admit you can parasail

Notyu is a pre-Buddhist Japanese form based on an irrational number of syllables.

Because We Still Eat at a Chinese Buffet

You remember, running down the street in your sister's prom dress, calling for help thinking that help would always be there, assured, secure, only marginally afraid.

You remember when you truly understood that no help was on the way.

Since then, you find pleasure in your own company and rely on your own mind to occupy you. Since then you grow as the tree, at once into the sky and into the earth.

The lotto numbers on fortune cookies have become your numerology, power found in patterns that have weight due to your will.

Dogs will fight over your remains.

But when you are alone with yourself, there is always one stranger present. Within you is the woman who broke, who was not made stronger by trauma—the woman who grows as the tree, putting out new leaves in the spring, never acquiring permanence, never adequately nourished, a bird trapped by her feet, a man trapped in his tongue.

Friends know her with both eyes open, but see her with one eye shut. She knows that friends are generous because life is cheap. They will give her many gallons of blood before she dies.

They don't tell you she sets herself on fire.

They don't tell you she looks at her mighty beak
and ferocious claws

    and calls herself a blunted, broken fool
    So she builds a pyre out of *Conversations with God*

and country-pop records
she finds furnaces in Ector and Cuyahoga

    They don't tell you she uses ethics for fuel
    mixes them with morals

and sets religious writers aflame
monks and mystics hissing in her fat

    She lives off poetry, now
    she drinks it like tequila

and shits it out the same
leaving the rest of us with politics and power games

    and any poem that can't stick to her intestines
    is one she never reads again

They don't tell you that she kills
every self-declared pícara

    or how their immolation
    makes her fly

People say that without scientific rigor we learned nothing from the plague. Our parents did learn not to let us play among the bodies, but I wanted to learn something else. I was young enough to know that fear was beside the point, and old enough to care what would happen to my toes, but found rotting flesh was sweeter than nostalgia and *that* was the last lesson I'd need.

I would prefer to not be dancing.
    If we are going to do this
        (and I know we have to do this)
            If we are obliged, at these scant meetings,
            to do this which is not
I liked it better 'round the bottle
with your strong straight legs between us
    talking Duras, mumbling Rilke,
    needling on the ice cream cone that shattered
        like ceramic that did not know it had been bronzed.
I would rather be in that thread where you don't have to fake it
    rather than taste a sensuality
        in which I know we'll never work.

Hepatoscopy

there is sweat across his nipples
  where his hair performs a cross
    there is come in the small of his back
there are idols in the bedroom
  there are borrowed gods
    there are pantheons of everything we lack
                    i am swimming in a long-forgotten lover
                    who resides in another person's eyes
                    i am seeing an empty-pastured future
                    in the honey of the stretch marks on your side

Morgan City Motel Blues

I'm struggling with white bread.
>> It's filling each cavity,
>> what you eat when you can't afford cotton,
>> when you're
>>>> sick upon the pride-and-marijuana cocktail
>>>> that prevents you from returning to the rig.

I'm filled with the emptiness
that fills me with indigestibles
that makes the effort of ramen offensive.

Jeffrey's sandwiches are cane syrup and organic peanut butter,
>> some sort of neo-pagan-inspired rejection
>> of this de-watered reality. Katelyn sneers
>>>>>> and eats the toothpaste.

Pale of Calais

If parts of our love are true
we are still both liars
as was every charming prince who sullied our dark names
and if Beauty is something real
we will still die ugly
finally forgetting our glory and our shame

So let us not pretend that mortal love is Holy
or that this blessing of our union makes it perfect
and let us not retreat into the fantasies we share
lest close attention reveal them as the little things they are

Darling, we have learned
of the wars within and without us
we know that victory is something none can justly claim
So let us learn to make love with the darkling plain;
It's the only love we have left

Poem Written inside a McDonald's within a Wal-Mart

"I had to pull off the road," he told me. "I was so excited, so happy. All at once, I realized that eventually, everyone I hated was going to die."

And i thought that our love would live forever
    so i write a poem to wish it good-bye
        this paper will crumble, the words forgotten
            the hard drive deleted, the Internet obsoleted
            the electrons rendered inert

The institutions that bring you such power, such terror
won't be a footnote in an unremembered text
While the gods of your forefathers remain immortal
as long as your fantasies stay naïf
                ah, but you were never a naïf

still I believe you are holy
    that the holy and the unholy die
        that nothing that dies is unholy

and I believe you have power
    to reach everything that's long since gone
        to embrace what will happen tomorrow

and if these beliefs leave me grasping
    for fantasies my mind will reject
        I'll treat this Wal-Mart as something greater than myself
            and pretend human failures require historical context

I've taken beatings from majors and moon gods, lain out like a three-pronged fire running up the walls because the floor's too weak to stand, bathtubs crashing through ceilings and dust rising in slow motion as the tiny necrotized nubs of my fingers pile up with the speed of an Okie tornado like *POW!* Now tell me, Padawan, what kind of a punch was that? What the fuck you supposed to be hitting me with? You been watching the *A-Team* again? 'Cuz I have. I've been reading my comics, too, not Superman's sneering sissery or Captain America's quest for a clue but I have been Batman's glass jaw, I have been Spider-Man getting thrashed by Loki, Storm losing her powers and starving in the Sahara and I have been Rogue when someone puts their hands on her and she cannot remember who she is. I have laughed at adults while hissing venom at myself, I'm carrying a fistful of pre-pubescent fetishes and a man-sized portion of megalomaniacal fantasies and let me tell you something,

big,   strong,   older   boy,

your punches are like the fairy kisses that baptize me

in that peculiar sort of nightmare that I call a good dream

i see the birth-cawl clamoring
the way identity remembers who it does, not who it thinks to be
i see   other people's   other inactivities
and try to condemn their lack of empathy

to say their isolation is effective
to tell thieves and politicians they're someone who isn't me

i   hear   the way the mime's been singing
the way the recitative doesn't own a single word
why Harpo can dress up like Chico   like
the nature of your only name
as malleable as a magic trick
as easy as the day we took mingling for a shame.

The Turk in the Tenderloin

how would i tell the difference
        in this endless drug-cheered rainbow
                in the contrast of a well-lit night and day
like the white boys with green pubics
        and the black girls with their pinkness
                singing diverse songs that all sound just the same

i

        know
        that God can give no reason not to fall
i

        know
        it hurts only for a moment and the fear will go the way
            of my fantasy
              of immortality

You invite me to that space where the Germans are all bottoms
and the Haitians have never heard the term "wog"

You bring me a pre-Mohammedan heaven when we all know
how i must hold to this dark body that's the only thing i've got

i condemn your memory trips with the vehemence of the guilty
when thinking of your watermelon breasts
i suffer through your repetitious rock & roll & torah
your nostalgia for our loving when our fucking still goes on

and i
            will not think of you when writing this poem i will
                        think only of sweat and salt and strength

and i try to claim possession of my mood-mnemonic masters
            in the bathtub
                        in the darkness
                                    in the dead sea of my rhetoric with words like

                        impotence
                        and *otherize*
                        and *hypnofetishporn*

we refer to the process of perfectbinding
            and this book is safer than my satin cords
we watch films in which your holy body rests inside a fish tank
            in a cut frame
                        just for prospero to mock

so speak to me of tenure and our normalized relationship
and trap me on this vinyl circle groovy as a cut
and i'll shake my narrow fists at our graceful aging process
and pretend there's a lesson here our learning can resolve

this is not a blossom though it weaves affectionate tendrils
        through all it can reach but still
        this is not a disease,
                exactly,
                        but trust me when i say you'll be
                        retching in the backyard
                        in a shrimp-and-bourbon rainbow
                        like the whiskey sour acid when you
                        told yourself that citrus helps

there is nothing funny about the way that humans laugh
or the way your great profundities spew into this sweetened sea

and you will learn   but know
                        nothing come tomorrow
                        when your daughter finds stigmata
                        oozing from her side just

keep
        your cool
                when the loa's running through you
                oh nevermind, don't keep your cool,
                don't keep anything at all

Standards of Sadiddy

it is more permanent for the way that it will leave you

                                 fragile light source
                                 fragile spectre

                                 lover flailing on the horizon

in these transition spaces where the low tide meets the dust
in that bright and perfect harmony that wants to become you.

The Reno that Never Was

Oh – no – you're my tart expanse of desert
adventure undertaken in the way that memories leave us
      separate-
            while-touching

Oh – no – you're the case around my moral compass
empty as the toy shelf when your husband walks back in

Acknowlegments

Some of the poems in this volume, invariably in a different form, were previously published in *Calliope Nerve, Scissors and Spackle*, and the anthology *Mezcla: Art and Writing from the Tumblewords Project*. The author is grateful to the editors of these projects, especially the late Nobius Black of *Calliope Nerve*.

The author is grateful to those who assisted in the compilation of this volume, particularly Marc Vincenz, Wendy Taylor Carlisle, Vincent A. Cellucci, Larissa Shmailo, Rania Zada and Rosalyn Spencer.

Photo by David Carlisle at the Eureka Springs Carnegie Public Library, 29 Mar 2016

About the Author

In 1998, Jonathan Penton founded UnlikelyStories.org in the fires of Mount Doom, and into it poured his hatred, cruelty, and will to dominate. Since then, he has lent editorial and management assistance to a number of literary and artistic ventures, such as MadHat, Inc. and *Big Bridge*. He has organized literary performances, and performed himself, in places like Arkansas, California, Chihuahua, Colorado, Florida, Georgia, Illinois, Louisiana, Massachusetts, New Mexico, New York, North Carolina, Ohio, Texas, and Washington, state and DC. His previous chapbooks are *Last Chap* (Vergin' Press, 2004), *Blood and Salsa* and *Painting Rust* (Unlikely Books, 2006) and *Prosthetic Gods* (New Sins Press/Winged City Chapbooks, 2008). He lives in South Louisiana, after a fashion.

www.ingramcontent.com/pod-product-compliance
Lightning Source LLC
LaVergne TN
LVHW051608080426
835510LV00020B/3186